An Encouraging WORD

LUANN DUNNUCK

CREATION
HOUSE PRESS
A STRANG COMPANY

AN ENCOURAGING WORD by Luann Dunnuck
Published by Creation House Press
A Strang Company
600 Rinehart Road
Lake Mary, Florida 32746
www.creationhouse.com

Unless otherwise noted, all Scripture quotations are from the New King James Version of the Bible. Copyright © 1979, 1980, 1982 by Thomas Nelson, Inc., publishers. Used by permission.

Scripture quotations marked NIV are from the Holy Bible, New International Version. Copyright © 1973, 1978, 1984, International Bible Society. Used by permission.

Scripture quotations marked NLT are from the Holy Bible, New Living Translation, copyright © 1996. Used by permission of Tyndale House Publishers, Inc., Wheaton, IL 60189. All rights reserved.

Cover design by Terry Clifton

Library of Congress Control Number: 2004112415
International Standard Book Number: 1-59185-715-5

04 05 06 07 08— 987654321
Printed in the United States of America

Dedication

Bob, thank you for being so patient
and compassionate.
You have waited for me to see the Son
shine through my clouds.

To my parents, thank you for
instilling principles of grace and wisdom
in my life. I will always honor you.

To my children, you continue to
inspire and add beauty to my life.
You are God's greatest gifts to me.

Acknowledgments

S AVINA, I WOULD like to thank you and your family for being a great source of encouragement to me in my younger years.

To Ginny at Creation House Press, thank you for answering all my e-mail concerns and questions. Where would we be without this technology?

To Rebecca, thank you for allowing me the time to write this book. You should be put in the employer hall of fame.

Contents

Introduction

AN ENCOURAGING WORD is something we all need to hear. The title of this book is the result of a conversation I had with a friend. That conversation helped changed my perspective on a problem I was facing. It is my goal for this book to be like a good friend on the other end of a telephone, giving you an encouraging word for your situation. Everyone needs to be encouraged.

I want to cheer you on to expect the good out of life. Jesus extends an invitation to you right now.

> Ho! Everyone who thirsts, Come to the waters; and you who have no money, come, buy and eat. Yes, come, buy wine and milk without money and without price, why do you spend

> money for what is not bread, and your wages
> for what does not satisfy? Listen carefully and
> eat what is good, and let your soul delight itself
> in abundance. Incline your ear to me and come
> to me.
>
> —ISAIAH 55:1–3

Are you desperate for a real change? Are you thirsty for a new perspective on life? Jesus is available to you with promises of joy and peace. Trust in His unfailing love and direction for your life. It is impossible for you to fail with God on your side. Just this morning I was in church and I was reminded that I needed to see myself as God sees me. I needed to be reminded not to look at myself through the eyes of my shortcomings, or through the eyes of those around me, but through the eyes of a loving God.

The greatest source of encouragement for anyone is the Bible, the words of God. I have found the Scriptures encouraged me when life came crashing in on all sides. I lived for many years with situations that threatened my well being. During that time God began to teach me ways to stay encouraged. I have outlined obstacles that I had to overcome in order to achieve peace. There are tools in this book that will help you defeat discouragement and help you defeat a temptation to despair. I have ended each chapter with a "notes" page. This is designed for the purpose of allowing you to write special thoughts you may have about the chapter. If a certain scripture or idea speaks to you, write it down in the notes section at the end of the chapter. This will enable you to remember important steps you need to take to live an encouraged life!

I enjoy my life now. I was recently thanking God for all that He has done in my life and all that He has brought me through. Many times I have fallen back into the arms of an ever-present, loving God. It is my prayer that this book will prevent you from wasting over a decade (like I did) from living a defeated life.

I have learned that I needed to change my habit of thinking. I used to quickly point out the negative side of a problem and dwell on how bleak and dismal my life was. Now I seek out the good in every situation, I seek out a successful solution, and I seek out help from a caring God.

How do you spend most of your days? Are you weighed down by the cares of this world, or are you expecting your trials to turn into your triumphs? Are you looking forward to your tomorrows or do you dread what the future has in store for you? I wrote this book to cheer you on! It is my intention to help you recognize that the best is yet to come! Hang in there and don't give up!

> Every dark day ends with a sunrise!
> Every tormenting night will eventually turn
> into a glorious morning!
> Every rainy day will always produce growth!
> Everything creation of God is capable of great
> success!

Don't Quit

When things go wrong, as they sometimes
    will,
When the road you're trudging seems all
    uphill,
When the funds are low and the debts are
    high,
And you want to smile, but you have to sigh,
When care is pressing you down a bit,
Rest if you must, but don't you quit.

Often the struggler has given up,
When he might have captured the victor's cup;
And he learned too late when the night came
    down,
How close he was to the golden crown.

Success is failure turned inside out,
The silver tint of the clouds of doubt,
And you never can tell how close you are,
It may be near when it seems so far;
So stick to the fight when you're hardest hit,
It's when things seem worst that you mustn't
    quit!

—Anonymous

I have come that they may have life, and that they may have it more abundantly.

—JOHN 10:10

CHAPTER 1

Your Quality of Life

W HAT *IS* YOUR quality of life? Do you enjoy the life God has given you? What if what I'm about to tell you is the absolute, undeniable truth? What if this bit of information could change your quality of life? What if I told you it is possible to live an encouraged life despite difficult circumstances? We all need to hear an encouraging word. Listen.

1. The trial you have been facing will become your greatest stepping stone.

2. Your pain will heal.

3. Your emotional struggle will turn into a powerhouse of strength for you.

4. Your loved one will one day cease to break your heart.

5. Your addiction will dismantle.

6. The raging crisis will settle down.

7. Your financial burden will be supplied.

8. Your aspiration or dream will be attained.

9. Your broken relationship will be healed.

10. You can lose weight.

11. You will come out of depression.

12. You do have tremendous value and worth.

13. You will find comfort even in the loss of your loved one.

14. Anything is possible if you believe.

The problem you are facing will pass. Be encouraged. Seasons always change. They do not stay the same all twelve months of the year, and our lives operate in the same way. If you are dissatisfied with the quality of your life just hang in there because your season can change for the better.

> *The problem you are facing will
> pass. Be encouraged. Seasons
> always change.*

I spent over a decade in a situation that could have left me emotionally bankrupt. I had to apply some of those statements from above to my situation. I had to remind myself that if I stayed the course I would see the sun shine again. And I did.

The quality of my life has changed. Although it is not perfect, it is filled with joy and peace. I have learned keys to recover that which has been stolen from me, and the greatest key is having a relationship with Jesus Christ. He promises us that He will never fail or forsake us, and His promises come to pass.

BITTERNESS

There may be some of you out there who are mad at God for your circumstances. Perhaps you feel like God could have stepped in and helped, but He didn't. I know, I have felt this way myself. There have been a handful of times I cried out to God with bitter tears. I felt that if God would have only stepped in, things would have been different. I can only tell you this is part of the human experience. Sometimes God has a very different plan for our lives, and in times of great tragedy we learn to trust in a loving God. I can't explain why your loved one died, why your marriage ended in divorce, or why you lost your job. There are some questions that won't be answered until we get to heaven. We are left with a life to live despite tragedies. How are we going to spend the rest of this life?

In my own life, I have experienced the death of a loved one very dear to me. It was very painful. It took a great deal of time for me to grieve over this death. But I have accepted this death. Although there are times when I miss that person (and I do allow myself to miss them), I don't get depressed over this situation any longer. I know that person is in heaven, and I believe that person is cheering me on to continue living a successful life.

I can tell you that God does not desire evil for your life. He does not desire that you spend the rest of your life in despair. There are numerous times in the Bible where godly people went through great difficulties, but in the end they were redeemed from their troubles. And this is what has happened in my life. Eventually those bitter tears turned into tears of joy. Eventually there was a joy in my heart that put laughter on my lips.

THE DEFINITION OF ENCOURAGEMENT

What does it mean to be encouraged? Noah Webster's 1828 edition of the *American Dictionary of the English Language* defines it this way: "to give or increase confidence of success;" "to inspire with courage, or strength of mind;" "to embolden;" "furnishing ground to hope for success;" and "as an encouraging prospect."[1] Now, what if your life was based on this definition? What if your life was headed in the direction of success? It is possible. I want to encourage you to begin thinking that success is possible for you. Success may be different for different people, but my definition of success is, walking out God's divine, inspired, anointed, and creative plan for your life. When we are walking in His divine plan for our lives, then we are successful and fulfilled.

I can already hear some of you making a case about the problems you are facing and how this will prevent you from living an encouraged life. If you have a relationship with Jesus Christ, then you can overcome your problems. While listening to a sermon by John Maxwell on miracles, I heard him say that after he studied every miracle in the Old and New Testament he found one common denominator in all of them: *a problem*. If you have problems in your life and you are tempted to say that you can't reach success in your life because of problems, then you are a prime candidate for a miracle. There is hope. A successful life is possible!

ENCOURAGEMENT FOR EVERYDAY LIFE

Another purpose for this book is to encourage you in your everyday life. One Fourth of July weekend my family and I were getting ready to get on a plane. The news media was bombarding the airwaves with news of terrorist threats. Even my husband (who is not worried by much) was a little cautious about flying on this particular weekend. So there we were excited about a vacation when all of a sudden we were faced with this looming threat of terror hanging over our heads. My attitude was "when it's my time to go I will not be able to avoid it, so why let terror steal my peace." I don't say that lightly. This comes from a woman who had dealt extensively with worry and anxiety. The big difference in my life is that I am now able to encourage myself. We all have to walk through life. We cannot avoid life's curves, but we can avoid making ourselves miserable.

Sources of Encouragement

The greatest source of encouragement is the promises found in the Word of God—the Bible. I believe this so strongly that I have dedicated an entire chapter to helping you personalize some of these promises for your life. They are the backbone of my life and have become a foundation whereby I draw strength. For example in Jeremiah 29:11 God says to you, "For I know the thoughts that I think toward you…thoughts of peace and not of evil, to give you a future and a hope." We learn from this one promise that God's plan for our lives is one of peace and one of a good future. This is encouraging news, and there are hundreds of other promises just like this one.

The people around you can determine the kind of encouragement you receive. Surrounding yourself with people who will help point you toward godly success will help you to stay encouraged. When I was younger I was often told not to hang around the wrong people or they will bring me down. The same principle applied when I became an adult. The key is to surround yourself with people that will cheer you on, people who are not threatened by your aspirations and dreams, and people who want to see you succeed.

Be an encourager to someone else. Find people whose lives you can speak encouragement into. Don't be shy about telling someone they did a good job, or that you appreciate them, or that their dreams are possible. For parents, this is something we can do for our children that can really make a difference in their lives. And remember, what you sow into other people's lives will be sown back into yours!

Christian books and music are also good, uplifting sources of encouragement. I do not like to watch a movie if it has a discouraging ending. I am not saying this is for everyone, but it has helped me. The apostle Paul said that "whatever things are of good report, if there is any virtue and if there is anything praiseworthy—meditate on these things" (Phil. 4:8). I have chosen to fill my mind with good things. How we feel is directly affected by what we are thinking. So in order to change how we feel we must first change how we think!

Lastly, after finding encouragement from God through the Bible, other people, and Christian books and music, I have learned to encourage *myself*. In 1 Samuel 30:1–6 we read an account where King David and all his men went back to the town where their wives and children lived only to find devastation. Their wives and their children were taken captive, and their enemies had burned down their city. The Bible tells us that David and his men "wept... until they had no more power to weep" (v. 4). These men were overwhelmed and distraught. Can you imagine coming home to find your loved ones taken prisoner? To make matters worse David's men blamed him for this calamity and even considered stoning him. However, the Bible says, "David strengthened himself in the Lord his God" (v. 6). There have been many times I have had to strengthen myself in the Lord. I have had to remind myself of His promises, pick myself up, and encourage myself with the truth that everything was going to work out for my good. When we encounter a fork in the road, we can choose to either encourage ourselves or to wallow in self-pity. Which path would you choose? Again I ask you, what do you want your quality of life to be?

A DAILY DECISION

Finding encouragement and joy is not based on outward circumstances. There are problems that arise that need our attention, but that doesn't mean we have to become or stay discouraged. The Bible tells us that the rain falls on the just and the unjust, and if we live long enough we will all get rained on. However, I want to encourage you to hang in there long enough to see the clouds part and the sun shine again.

I can look back on my life (as I'm sure you can, too) and recall desperate situations. These problems either worked themselves out or God intervened and straightened out what I could not fix. I am encouraged today to know that the same thing can happen in my current situation. I have greatly improved the quality of life that I lead because I have changed my thinking. This good news comes from someone who has wasted many years focusing on the wrong things.

You have the choice to find something to be joyful about, something to look forward to, and Someone (Jesus) to rejoice in! Begin today. Start changing your quality of life. If I can go from being extremely negative and worrying myself into a panic attack, you can begin to change the way you think, too. In John 10:10 Jesus says, "I have come that they may have life, and that they may have it more abundantly." Let's begin to daily walk in that abundant life!

I encourage you to write down all the good things that you have in your life right now. Be daring enough to write down all of your obstacles and problems, and bring them to God in prayer. Begin to believe God for a miracle, begin to believe in God's goodness to you, and begin to expect your circumstances to change.

NOTES

Death and life are in the power of the tongue.

—Proverbs 18:21

CHAPTER 2

You Are What You Speak

BEFORE WE GO any further, I want to show you how every day we either choose to curse or bless ourselves with what we say and think. Our words and our thoughts greatly impact our daily lives. The Bible has a great deal to say on this subject. The good news is that this is an area we can easily control. So often we berate and second-guess ourselves in our thoughts or in our words. I want to break this down in two areas: 1) our thoughts and 2) our speech.

We Are What We Think

We need to be cautious in our thinking. Proverbs 23:7 says, "For as he thinks in his heart so is he." If you think of yourself as someone who lives an encouraged peaceful life, you probably will live that way. If you see yourself as never measuring up to the next person, or always failing at anything you try, you will probably be frustrated and quit before you succeed. When I first began writing I would often think, *I can't do this. I don't know anything about writing.* However, the more I began to write the more confidence I began to have. My thinking started to change in this area, and I began to believe in myself and my newfound ability to write. But the lesson here is *if* I had given up and *if* I remained negative I would have missed out on the gift of writing.

> *If you think of yourself as someone who lives an encouraged peaceful life, you probably will live that way.*

Our thinking begins like a seed. We get a negative thought in our mind. Next we meditate and dwell on that negative thought over and over again. Finally we speak that negative thought out and it becomes an action. The same is true of a positive thought. We get a positive thought, and we meditate on that thought, until finally it becomes an action. It can work either way. I have found from personal experience my mind was trained very keenly to focus on the negative.

When I began to change my negative thoughts into positive uplifting thoughts, I found it initially to be a struggle. My habit was to think in a very self-defeating manner. I came across this life-changing commentary that deserves repeating. This excerpt is taken from *Thinking for a Change* by John C. Maxwell.[1]

> I am your constant companion. I am your greatest helper or heaviest burden. I will push you onward or drag you down to failure.
>
> I am completely at your command. Half of the things you do you might just as well turn over to me and I will be able to do them quickly and correctly.
>
> I am easily managed—you must merely be firm with me. Show me exactly how you want something done and after a few lessons I will do it automatically.
>
> I am the servant of all great men; and alas, of all failures as well. Those who are great I have made great. Those who are failures, I have made failures.

I am not a machine, though I work with all the
precision of a machine plus the intelligence of
a man.

You may run me for profit or run me for ruin—
it makes no difference to me.

Take me, train me, be firm with me, and I will
place the world at your feet. Be easy with me
and I will destroy you.

Who am I? I am a habit!

—ANONYMOUS

There is tremendous wisdom in this excerpt. Because
our brains do not know the difference between a good
habit and a bad one, we need to train our minds to think
victoriously and then our mouths will speak victoriously.
The only way to change a bad habit is to replace it with
something good. This takes time and repetition. I can honestly tell you that when I begin to think negatively now, it
just doesn't feel right. That is because I am enjoying my
newfound freedom to think encouraging thoughts.

I have learned that our thoughts directly affect how we
feel. The reason we are feeling angry, fearful, or depressed
is because we are thinking in an angry, fearful, or depressed
way. The only way to change how we feel is to begin to
change what we think about.

When something is bothering me, I will think on the
situation over and over again. What I have to do is dis-

tract myself with something good. This works. If your thoughts are focused on a negative situation, change your focus to something positive. Once your mind is on the positive then your feelings will follow. Keep this in mind next time you are feeling bad. Ask yourself what you are thinking about that is causing you to feel down. Once you have identified what it is that is making you feel down, do what you can to fix the problem and leave the rest for God to work out. If you apply this principle to your life you will have peace, and you will live an encouraged life!

When I speak to women's groups, I will often tell them I like whom I see in the mirror these days, but this was *not* always the case. Negative discouraging thoughts would bombard my mind on a daily basis. I would dwell on all the things I was not and never would accomplish. For example I would tell myself, "I will never accomplish my goals." "I am not a good wife." "I've failed at . . ." "I can never . . ." The list was endless. I would dwell on the negative aspects of who I was. I would declare these statements out loud. I was cursing myself with my thoughts and my words. Now, if I start to go down that path of defeating thoughts, I quickly recognize what I'm doing and change the direction of my thoughts. I treat myself a little better these days, and it makes for a much happier life.

I encourage you to stop and write down what you are thinking about at various times of your day, or at least pay attention to what you are thinking about. If you are anything like me you are always thinking. The goal is to focus your thoughts on the good and leave the discouraging thoughts behind. This will greatly affect the quality of life you lead.

Time for Rest

There are times when we need to rest our minds. Psalm 46:10 says, "Be still, and know that I am God." Sometimes it is important to rest your mind and trust God. Go out and have fun, laugh, or go out and enjoy nature. Take a walk, do something fun, and let your mind rest. There comes a point when we need to trust God, and let go of our problems and worries. I am reminded of the biblical account of Creation in the first two chapters of Genesis.

> And God said, "Let there be light," and there was light....And God said, "Let the water under the sky be gathered to one place..." And it was so....Then God said, "Let the land produce vegetation..." And it was so....And God said, "Let the land produce living creatures according to their kinds..." And it was so....Then God said, "Let us make man in our image, in our likeness..." So God created man....God saw all that he had made, and it was very good....By the seventh day God had finished the work he had been doing; so on the seventh day he *rested* from all his work. And God blessed the seventh

day and made it holy, because on it he *rested* from all the work of creating that he had done.

—GENESIS 1:3–2:3, NIV, EMPHASIS ADDED

If God found it important enough to set aside some time for rest then we should learn from His example and do the same. I find when I don't take some time out to relax I become irritable and easily frustrated. I have learned to create some downtime for my family and me. There is wisdom in resting!

Sometimes when I'm trying to fall asleep my mind will start to problem solve. This is not the time to problem solve. This is a great skill to have but not at 11:00 at night. What helps my mind to relax is to visualize a passage from Psalm 23. It reads, "He makes me to lie down in green pastures; He leads me beside the still waters. He restores my soul" (vv. 3–4). I think on this scripture, and it helps me rest my thoughts and fall asleep. We all need to find some serenity and peace of mind.

WE ARE WHAT WE SPEAK

The average person does not realize the power of their words. Proverbs and James have much to say about the impact of our words.

Death and life are in the power of the tongue.

—PROVERBS 18:21

He who guards His mouth preserves his life.

—Proverbs 13:3

A man has joy by the answer of his mouth,
And a word spoken in due season, how good
it is.

—Proverbs 15:23

Whoever guards his mouth and tongue keeps
his soul from troubles.

—Proverbs 21:23

Look also at ships: although they are so large
and are driven by fierce winds they are turned
by a very small rudder wherever the pilot
desires. Even so the tongue is a little member
and boasts great things.

—James 3:4–5

We must be careful about what comes out of our
mouths because, as we have already learned, the thoughts
we think come out as words that have influence in our
lives. I simply want to make the connection that when we
speak something out loud it reinforces our thoughts thus
predicting our actions. This can work to our advantage
or to our disadvantage. For example, if someone needs
to lose weight and all they ever say is that they will never
lose weight, they are reinforcing the negative thought,
thus predicting the negative outcome of their situation. If a person says that they are struggling with their

weight but are determined to lose the weight and have confidence they will reach their goal, they probably will succeed. Take a moment right now to think of an area in your life where you are struggling. Now, say out loud both the positive and the negative concerning that situation. It actually feels better to be able to proclaim the positive, encouraging statement. It is very rare that I will say, "I am never going to..." or "I will never accomplish..." This is self-defeating and extremely discouraging. I do not want to curse my life. I want to speak blessing over myself and my family.

SEEDS OF LOW SELF-ESTEEM

There are several reasons why a person has low self-esteem. Some people were not affirmed and encouraged properly as children. Some believe they have done something so terrible they will never be good enough. Some people were made fun of by classmates in grade school, and this affects how they see themselves even now as adults. There are endless reasons why someone may have low self-esteem. But I want to encourage you as an adult to take responsibility for yourself. It is time to let go of the past. Start right now, today.

Promise yourself that you are going to begin to like yourself, no matter what you have or have not done. Remind yourself that God created you, and He is not in the business of making mistakes. Claim what the Word says about who you are.

I am fearfully and wonderfully made;
Marvelous are Your works,
And that my soul knows very well.
My frame was not hidden from You,
When I was made in secret,
And skillfully wrought in the lowest parts of
the earth.
Your eyes saw my substance, being yet
unformed.
And in Your book they were all written,
The days fashioned for me,
When as yet there were none of them.

—PSALM 139:14–16

God values you. He formed and fashioned you. It is very difficult for you to have low self-esteem when you know Jesus loves you so much that He was willing to die for your freedom. You must be worth a great deal for God to go through so much trouble.

Self-confidence is built over time. A great example of this is my husband. He is one of the most emotionally healthy people I have ever met (and there are not many out there). My husband has a great singing voice. I always told him so, but he never believed me. But the more he began to sing at church and in front of other people, the more people began telling him what a great voice he had. The point is when he began singing he had little confidence in his ability, but the more he practiced and performed the more his confidence grew. Now, (although he would never admit it because he is a very humble guy) he has a healthy self-confidence concerning his singing ability.

I encourage you to begin to like the person God has created you to be. It is important to realize, as I did, that disliking yourself is an insult to God. You are His precious child, and until you begin to like yourself you will not be able to speak or think encouragement into your life. This is not an overnight process, but it is important to start somewhere. If I can accomplish changing my view of myself, so can you!

Take a few moments now to write down your positive characteristics and qualities. And by the way, it is OK to write down your negative qualities (we all have them) and bring them to God in prayer. Ask Him to help you change and become the person He created you to be.

NOTES

_____

_____

_____

_____

_____

_____

_____

_____

_____

_____

_____

_____

_____

_____

There is therefore now no condemnation
to those who are in Christ Jesus...

—ROMANS 8:1

CHAPTER 3

You Deserve to Be Guilt Free

W̲E WERE GETTING ready to purchase our second home. Since we had this home built, I was able to choose countertops, cabinets, flooring, and so on. This was such an exciting time, but there was just one problem. I did not feel like I deserved this home. When God would bless me with good things, I would get this I-don't-deserve-it complex.

During those months when we were building our home, I stumbled upon a scripture in Proverbs that reads, "The blessing of the Lord makes one rich, and He adds no sorrow with it" (10:22). I want to focus on the second half of that verse: "He adds no sorrow with it." When God pours out blessings on us, He does not want us to give the gift

33

back and say, "Thank you, but I really don't deserve this gift." Much like if you were to give your child a gift and that child handed it back to you and said, "I don't deserve anything good. I'm sorry I can't accept it." This seems like an absurd concept, yet some of us do this because we don't feel good enough to receive.

When God pours out blessings on us, He does not want us to give the gift back and say, "Thank you, but I really don't deserve this gift."

Why do some of us have this problem of feeling like we don't deserve good things to happen in our lives? I can only tell you from personal experience why I had trouble receiving good things from God. 1) I struggled with severe guilt, 2) there were certain sins in my life that I felt I needed to spend the rest of my life paying for, and 3) I did not know how to receive forgiveness on a daily basis.

I am going to spend the rest of this chapter dealing with these three areas. I pray you are set free as I was.

GUILT

Guilt from yesterday can rob us from the blessings of today. The enemy of our soul uses guilt to steal any happiness that tries to come our way. There are many sources of guilt. For me it was feeling guilty over several events that happened in my life. Some of those events I had no control over. One such event was my parents' divorce. I was a child when they divorced and I thought the divorce was my fault. No one ever *told* me it was my fault, but as a child I interpreted it this way. The Lord showed me over a period of time that this wrong view scarred my thinking as an adult. Throughout most of my adult life I did not even realize that I had guilty feelings over this event. But I came to understand that this divorce was not my fault. I accepted this truth and began to live my life free from this misbelief.

I remember reading a book and the words *not guilty* jumped off the page. I thought, *I'm not feeling particularly guilty about* anything, why are these words *beaming off the page at me?* I began to pray and ask the Lord why these words were standing out. He showed me a scene from my childhood when my mother was being physically abused by her husband. He showed me that somehow I took on the responsibility of protecting her and that I felt guilty because I was not able to keep her safe. Realistically, I was only a child and was unable to protect her. But I still felt guilty. It was a feeling I was not aware of, yet it had a great impact on my life. If someone asked me as an adult if I felt guilty because I was not able to protect my mother, I would have said of course not. Yet down deep I did feel guilty, and it affected me. In order to gain the victory over this feeling, I had to once again replace a lie with the truth. The truth is that I am not guilty because I did not do any harm. Eventually, I accepted this truth, and I no longer carry hidden guilt over these situations. I thank God for having been so gracious to me to show me where I was bound, so that I could be set free.

Sometimes there are deeper hurts in our lives that show themselves in peculiar ways. The Holy Spirit is the best Counselor, because He knows the deep scars that we carry. My life has been like an onion. Layer by layer God has showed me how I took on guilt that was never mine to carry. This wrong thinking prevented me from living an encouraged life.

LET GO

The second area I want to focus on is past mistakes. These mistakes are sins we chose to participate in, and now we deeply regret having done them. There were certain sins that I knowingly partook in, but many years later I felt a strong sense of condemnation because of those mistakes. I spent almost ten years feeling guilty over events that happened in my life. I felt as though I should spend the rest of my life paying for my mistakes.

I had knowledge of God and a relationship with God, yet I still felt condemned. I knew all the right scriptures and all the facts of salvation, yet I still felt as though I needed to pay a price for my sins. There were things I did in my life that haunted me, and I did not even realize it. I have found that when we commit wrong acts, we stuff them in the bottom of our souls. Every once in a while those wrong acts will come up and torment us.

I recently read from an old journal of mine and noticed a way of thinking that I used to have; I wrote, "I must be the worst Christian in the world. I bring God no joy because of my weakness. God is always disappointed and frustrated with me." When I read this now, I cannot believe how wrong my view of God was. The opposite is true. God's love is unconditional. I am not the worst Christian in the world because of my weakness. God is never disappointed and frustrated with me when I'm trying to overcome weakness. I was surprised to read how hard I was on myself for my past mistakes. What lies I believed back then! Being stuck in so much guilt and condemnation is what robbed me from enjoying my life.

Step number one to being free of this cycle is to admit you did it. "Yes, I did…Yes, I feel terrible that I did…I wish I could go back and do things differently." Then talk to somebody about this wrongdoing or write about it until it does not bother you anymore. Next, take responsibility for your actions. Do not play the blame game. No one forced you to do what you did. You acted of your free will. Then grieve over it. Grieve over the pain it has caused you or the pain you may have caused someone else. This is such an important step not to be overlooked. This step may take time, counseling, or sharing with a good friend. Then go to God in prayer and ask Him to forgive you of this wrongdoing. I imagine a forgiven stamp being stamped over my sins. This helps it sink in that I am truly forgiven. I remember hearing a friend tell me if God could forgive the apostle Paul for murdering Christians (before he had a relationship with Jesus), then He could forgive me.

Then finally, let it go. You do not have to emotionally beat yourself up any longer. God promises in Isaiah 1:18, "Come now, and let us reason together," says the Lord, "though your sins are like scarlet, they shall be white as snow." God is waiting for us to get past our past. He has a good future for us, but we cannot enjoy it if we are stuck in the past. If I can feel good about myself despite my mistakes, so can you. Not only do I feel good about myself, but I am also expecting God to do great things in and through my life.

In Isaiah 62:1–5 God says, "You shall be called by a new name, which the mouth of the Lord will name....You shall be called Hephzibah." *Hephzibah* literally means "My delight is in you."[1] God gives you a new name and a new nature. Although we may still sin, we are no longer condemned by sin. This took me a long time to really believe. But now I feel like I am God's favorite, and you should feel like you are God's favorite, too!

DAILY FORGIVENESS

Are you ready for some startling information? You are not perfect. And neither am I. That is why God knew we would have to go to Him daily and ask for a fresh start. Joyce Meyer has this saying that has become my life motto.

I even bought the coffee mug that says the same thing. It goes something like this: "I'm not where I want to be, but I'm not where I used to be. I'm on my way, and I'm OK." This is the truth that I have accepted. I have learned to give myself some breathing room. It is OK to try something and make a mistake. It is OK to fail as long as I get back up. The motive of my heart is never to intentionally hurt someone, but unfortunately my words or actions still hurt them. In times like these I need to go to that person, ask for forgiveness, and then go to God and ask Him for forgiveness. Finally I must receive this forgiveness by forgiving myself.

In Matthew 6:9–13—the Lord's Prayer—Jesus teaches us how to pray. Through this prayer, God reveals something special about His purpose of forgiveness in our lives. "Give us this day our daily bread, and forgive us our debts, as we forgive our debtors" (vv. 11–12). God knew we would need to cleanse our hearts daily. He knew that, in order for us to be emotionally healthy, we would have to let go of the wrongs we commit and the wrongs that are committed against us.

I used to feel very strongly that I did not deserve anything good from God because of all my mistakes. I would not accept what Jesus did on the cross for me two thousand years ago. I realize now this is an insult to God. Think about it. Jesus was beaten beyond recognition, suffered, and died so you and I can live free from the guilt of our sins. The Book of Isaiah says that He became a "guilt offering" for you and me. (See Isaiah 53:10, NIV) Yet we say to Him that it was not good enough. We inadvertently say to Him that we need to suffer for our mistakes. I love God too much to insult Him like this. So I accept His sacrifice and forgiveness. I no longer live under guilt and condemnation.

NEW MERCY TODAY

I can honestly say that it is very rare for me to spend a lot of time beating myself up emotionally anymore. It is a waste of time. I also stay clear of anyone who consistently teaches or preaches condemnation. Yes, God disciplines us, but He always redirects us in love. Lamentations 3:22–23 says, "Through the LORD's mercies we are not consumed, because His compassions fail not. They are new every morning; great is your faithfulness." Every morning we have the opportunity to start the day out right. God is compassionate and looks not only at what we do, but also why we do it. He looks at the scars of our heart, and He desires to heal us of those wounds. God's ability and willingness to forgive us is secure. I accept His invitation to live an encouraged guilt-free life.

VIEW OF GOD

My view of God has dramatically changed. I used to view God as ready to punish me for any little mistake. I pictured Him as being aloof, always wanting to teach me through difficult trials and tests, and never pleased with me. As you can gather from this description, my view of God was very inaccurate. I had an emotionally unhealthy relationship with God and a miserable existence.

Through time, this is what I came to know about God: God is compassionate, patient, and long-suffering. He desires to bless us with good things. He sees the potential He put in each of us. He smiles on us when He sees how hard we are trying. He loves us despite our weaknesses. And most of all, He gives us GRACE. The definition of *grace*, according to *Webster's 1828 Dictionary*, is "favor, good will, kindness, free unmerited love of God."[2] It is good to know that this is the view through which God sees us.

Although this is a much healthier view of God toward us, a lot of times our views of God are shaped by the role models in our lives. Perhaps a pastor, priest, or family member was a hard taskmaster. Because these people were significant authority figures in your life, you imagined that God must act that way also. But the best way to understand God's characteristics and to reshape your view of Him is to study the Bible. There, you will find a balance of who God is. You will find times when God had to deal sternly with His people, disciplining them for the greater good. You will also see many times when God is extremely merciful, long-suffering, and compassionate toward His people.

Jesus gives us a beautiful illustration of our heavenly Father's heart, "Or what man is there among you who, if his son asks for bread, will give him a stone? Or if he asks for a fish, will he give him a serpent? If you then, being evil, know how to give good gifts to your children, how much more will your Father who is in heaven give good things to those who ask Him!" (Matt. 7:9–11). Be encouraged to know God is for you, and He has a good plan for your life. Just relax in His arms.

Enjoy Your Life

Going back to my initial story of the new home. For the first year of living in the house, I would get on my knees and thank God for the new home. I never thought such a blessing would happen to me. I am still very grateful for this blessing, and I know that He desires that I enjoy future gifts from Him. Similarly, be ready to enjoy the blessings He has in store for you. I encourage you to hold your head up high and know that you have been forgiven and cleansed of your past mistakes. You were worth dying for. He died that you might live, and He wants you to enjoy your life.

NOTES

Hope deferred makes the heart sick.

—PROVERBS 13:12

CHAPTER 4

Are You Hopeful?

A RE YOU LOOKING forward to something good to happen in your life? Are you hopeful that your current problem will be resolved? We all need to have hope. We stay encouraged by hoping and expecting a good outcome for our lives. The opposite of hope is despair. I believe having hope is a key to emotional well-being, which is why I have decided to dedicate an entire chapter to *hope*.

Webster's 1828 Dictionary defines *hope* as "a desire of some good, accompanied with at least a slight expectation of obtaining it, or a belief that it is obtainable. Confidence in a future event; the highest degree of well founded expectation of good; as a hope founded on God's gracious promises."[1] I want to encourage you to begin to hope again. If you once believed in a dream or a good outcome for yourself and you have lost hope in that dream, begin to hope in a good future. Get excited again, begin to believe again, raise your level of expectation, and whatever you do don't give up, we all need to look forward to something good.

When we don't have any hope we can get depressed. Proverbs 13:12 says, "Hope deferred makes the heart sick." God knew that when we have no hope, our feelings, our will, our intellect would be sick. When we hope, we become strong. When we are confident that our outcome will be good, we stay encouraged. The opposite is true also. When we have no hope for our situation, we become hopeless, which can lead to depression. If you observe someone who is suicidal, you will find that they have lost hope. Hope gives us motivation to continue on despite difficult circumstances. I have seen, in my own life and in the life other people, dire circumstances turn around for the good. If we don't hang in there through the struggle we will never know the joy that is on the other side of that struggle.

When we hope, we become strong.

A Pregnant Woman

Just as a pregnant woman is confident in her expectation of having a baby, we should have the same kind of expectation for God's promises to be fulfilled in our lives. We may not be able to see or touch the promises, but we should be confident that they will come to pass. Set your mind on the surety of what you have been expecting. Be persistent if you have to. Be willing to be like a pregnant woman, knowing beyond any doubt that what you are hoping for will come into being.

There are several obstacles you could be facing. There may be problems that seem overwhelming to you right now, but I'm encouraging you to be hopeful. Believe that whatever your current problem is, it *will* work out. What are you facing right now? What is it that looks so impossible to you now? Whatever it is, believe that God will turn it around for your good, do what you know to do, and then rest.

Joseph's Story

People who cross over to the other side of their troubles are often people who were hopeful even when things were at their worst. One of my favorite people in the Bible to study is Joseph, the son of Jacob. I will try to summarize Joseph's life. (See Genesis 30–50.)

Joseph was given a gift from God to interpret dreams. In one of Joseph's dreams he saw his whole family bowing down to him. Joseph's brothers were so jealous of the dream and his gift that they sold him to a caravan that was passing by their fields. Joseph was taken away as a prisoner to a foreign land. He was forced to leave everything that was familiar to him and everything that he loved.

When Joseph got to Egypt, he was sold as a slave to Potiphar, an officer of Pharaoh. Although he was a slave, he prospered in all that he did. God's favor was with Joseph. Potiphar's wife made a pass at him. When Joseph rejected her advances, she lied to her husband and said that Joseph tried to seduce her. Joseph was then thrown into prison for a crime he did not commit.

He continued to prosper in prison. The prison guard put Joseph in charge of the other prisoners. Eventually through the interpretation of one of the prisoner's dreams, Joseph was called to interpret one of Pharaoh's dreams. Because Joseph correctly interpreted his dream, Pharaoh made him second in command of the entire nation of Egypt. Only Pharaoh was greater than Joseph. Joseph's interpretation of the dream predicted that there would be seven years of plenty in Egypt and seven years of famine. This came to pass just as Joseph had said, and God used Joseph to save Egypt and the surrounding cities from this famine. Joseph began to fulfill his purpose.

Joseph encountered his brothers when they came to Egypt to buy grain because of the famine. His brothers were shocked to see him, but Joseph encouraged them. He let them know that God sent him to Egypt to save the land from severe famine. He explained to them that what was meant for his evil God turned around for good. In the end Joseph forgave his brothers and was reconciled to them.

The point I want to make is Joseph had dreams and a purpose, but he had problems. Still he never gave up. He continued to walk out God's plan for his life despite his obstacles. He did not succumb to temptation. He pressed forward despite his life's getting worse before it got better. He had many opportunities to lose hope and become bitter with God. If Joseph had given up he would not have fulfilled God's purpose for his life.

My life has been a lot like Joseph in that I spent over a decade dealing with difficult obstacles. There were many times I wanted to quit, but there was this hope inside of my soul that kept me encouraged. Many times my situation appeared to get worse before it got better, but I hung in there. Whatever you are facing right now I encourage you to hang in there, too!

In difficult times we need to have hope to press forward. We need to lean on God and draw strength from Him to face our tomorrows. Pray, read your Bible, find a good church, and surround yourself with supportive people. Expect God to turn your situation around, and never lose hope.

Door of Hope

In Hosea 2:15 God says, "I will give her...a door of hope; she shall sing there, as in the days of her youth." In

Hebrew *hope* means "something yearned for and anticipated eagerly, something for which one waits, to look in a particular direction."[2] The word comes from the idea of stretching like a rope. Sometimes our faith is stretched like a rope. Have you ever felt this way? Have you ever felt as though everything in you is being stretched? The good news is there is One greater than us holding onto the other end of our rope. God has promised that He will never leave us or forsake us. He promises to never give us more than we can handle, and I believe that. The most hopeful and encouraging book you will ever read is the Bible.

I encourage you to walk through the door of hope, because on the other side of that door of hope is your answer. Keep anticipating your need to be fulfilled, and be confident that everything is going to work out in your life just as it did for Joseph. Life is too short to stay discouraged.

"What-if-ing"

Negative "what-if-ing" steals hope. For those of you who do not understand the concept of negative "what-if-ing," let me explain. This is when we start evaluating the negative possibilities. For example, imagine someone is having stomach pains. They begin to think to themself, *What if I have an ulcer? What if I have to have surgery because of this ulcer? What if my ulcer causes me to get stomach cancer? What if I die from the stomach cancer?* You get the picture. Their thinking process spiraled out of control for the worse and stole their hope.

We can also "what-if" the positive. This is evaluating the positive possibilities. I was preparing to get on an airplane. Immediately I began to think to myself, *What if I get on the plane and I find it very relaxing? What if meet someone whom I enjoy having a conversation with? What if when I land I have the best vacation ever? What if on vacation I get refreshed and feel rejuvenated?* The difference was remarkable. We can choose to analyze the positive, or we can dread an event and make ourselves miserable.

I have learned that to live an encouraged life I need to watch my "what-if-ing." I used to be really great at "what-if-ing" myself into a panic. I would focus on all the wrong things. My example earlier of flying is a great example because I used to spend weeks dreading getting on a plane. Now I enjoy flying because I know that my life is in God's hands. I know that when it is my time to go, it will not matter where I am. So why not enjoy the ride?

SEEK THE GOOD

To remain hopeful, I look for and seek after a positive outcome. How I feel emotionally is a choice I make every day. God gave us free will to choose to be hopeful or to choose to be discouraged. At the base of peace of mind is the belief that I will always be OK because God loves me enough to take good care of me. This foundational belief is extremely freeing. Even if you did not have a stable childhood or a stable adulthood, you can put your life in the hands of a stable God. He created you and will take good care of you. There is an endearing passage of Scripture found in Matthew 6:26–33. It says:

> Look at the birds of the air, for they neither sow nor reap nor gather into barns; yet your heavenly Father feeds them. Are you not of more value then they?...Consider the lilies of the field how they grow; they neither toil or spin; and yet I say to you even Solomon in all his glory was not arrayed like one of these.... Therefore do not worry, saying, "What shall we eat?" or "What shall we drink?" or "What shall we wear?"... Your heavenly Father knows that you need all these things. But seek first the kingdom of God and His righteousness, and all these things shall be added to you.

This is Jesus speaking to you and me. He is encouraging us to rest in the Father's care. He is teaching us that if God is able to take care of the birds of the air and the flowers in the field, surely He is able to take care of us. Rest in God.

NOTES

Your eyes saw my substance, being yet unformed. And in Your book they all were written, the days fashioned for me, when as yet there were none of them.

—Psalm 139:16

CHAPTER 5

Fulfilling Your Purpose

I T WAS CHRISTMASTIME 1994 when the Lord revealed
to me that I would one day write a book. My first book
was published in December 2003, nine years later. I
had a purpose, and I was going to see that purpose fulfilled in my life. I could write a whole other book on those
nine years. All that to say this: purpose kept me encouraged when everything around me was falling apart. Knowing that God had a specific purpose for me brought me
encouragement. This is another key to living an encouraged life. When a friend was trying to cheer me up during
a particularly turbulent time of my life, she told me about a
song that went something like this: the desire in your heart
is a confirmation that a destination is there. Basically this

means that even when you do not see how a dream will be fulfilled hang in there because God's will, coupled with your desire, can produce great things.

The definition of *purpose* is "that which a person sets before himself as an object to be reached or accomplished; the Supreme Being created intelligent beings for some benevolent and glorious purpose."[7] You have a purpose. God has placed in you a mission to accomplish. Sometimes we know what that assignment is and sometimes we just fall into our destiny by divine design. Either way it is good to know that our lives have meaning.

I have a friend who is an evangelist. He is fulfilling God's plan for his life. My neighbor is a teacher, and that is her purpose. I have a friend who is a state legislator in my state. I am confident that he is fulfilling the purpose in his life. We all have a purpose. We all have gifts. We all have God-given abilities that are unique to us. No one else could fulfill our destiny but us. Perhaps you feel your purpose is to be a good parent, police officer, or pharmacist. Maybe your goal is to make money in the business world to help support missionaries. The list could go on. Whatever it is, you have a destiny to fulfill.

Where Am I Going?

For those of you who do not know what your purpose is I encourage you to do some self-examining. Write down what you're good at and the things you enjoy doing. Write

56

down what you would do with each day if money was not an issue. What talent do you have that people compliment you on? Answering questions like these can help you discover what your God-given gifts and talents are. You can also find out what you should *not* be doing with your life by using this same process. Write down occupations that you know you would not be good at. Write down what abilities frustrate you and which subjects were never your favorites in school.

Some people already know what their purpose is, and they are making decisions that will accomplish those goals. If you are perplexed because you have not figured it out yet don't be discouraged. Begin to do some self-analysis, and begin to pray that God will reveal to you what He has placed you on this earth to do.

Your purpose in life should not be to see your name in lights. If that is what you are after check your motivations. I know some of the most helpful people who were always there with a helping hand. This is a tremendous gift of "helps." To be a support to someone is a talent. I can recall some presidential first ladies of the past who were great supports to their husbands while they were in office. If they were not supporting their husbands, some presidents would not have accomplished what they were put on this earth to do. I can assure you that whatever your purpose is, it will fit you like a hand in a glove. I am not saying everything comes easy to you when you are walking in your purpose, but your purpose is designed to fit you properly.

THE EXCUSE

Jeremiah was a prophet in the Old Testament. When God called him for a special purpose, Jeremiah told God he could not fulfill his assignment.

> Then the word of the LORD came to me saying: "Before I formed you in the womb I knew you; before you were born I sanctified you [cleansed you]; I ordained you a prophet to the nations." Then said I: "Ah Lord GOD! Behold I cannot speak, for I am a youth." But the LORD said to me: "Do not say, 'I am a youth,' for you shall go to all whom I send you, and whatever I command you, you shall speak. Do not be afraid of their faces, for I am with you to deliver you," says the LORD.
>
> —JEREMIAH 1:4–8

This is a great example of God commissioning someone to fulfill their destiny and that person using fear as an excuse to not live out their purpose.

Let's break this down. Before God told Jeremiah what his purpose was, God assured Jeremiah that He already knew him thoroughly. God knew his strengths, his weakness, his successes, and his failures, both past and future. So Jeremiah could have relaxed because God knew exactly whom He was calling. Next God told him that He sanctified him. The Hebrew meaning for *sanctified* is "to pronounce clean, to appoint, to keep holy, to purify." God was saying to Jeremiah He had already approved of him. God had looked at his resume and assured Jeremiah that he was the man for the job.

When God calls you to fulfill a job, rest assured God has all confidence that you can fulfill that job. Look at what Jeremiah's response back to God was, "I cannot speak; I am a youth." Jeremiah was saying, "I am not experienced enough. I don't feel adequate enough to do what you are asking me to do. I may not be good enough for this assignment." Jeremiah was afraid. But listen to what God's reply back to Jeremiah was, "Do not be afraid of their faces, for I am with you to deliver you." God reassured Jeremiah of His presence. Jeremiah needed to know that he had all the power of heaven on his side. That same power is here for us as we fulfill God's will for our lives. Jeremiah was no different than you and I today. Sometimes we need encouragement when we begin to walk in our purposes.

When God begins to point us to His will and plan for our lives, we sometimes come up with excuses why we cannot fulfill that plan. Many times what is behind those excuses is fear. I remember a time when I was getting ready to speak at a women's seminar, and I was very nervous. I kept reasoning in my mind, *You know you are called to speak to women, so why are you so afraid?* At that, I got another thought, *I approve of you.* Instantly I knew God was trying to tell me to relax and that I was good enough to be there. He had already checked out my resumé and knew I was the person He wanted there. With that assurance the nerves decreased, and I spoke with confidence. Sometimes the gift is resident within us, but we lack the confidence to fulfill our destiny. This is exactly what happened to Jeremiah, but God assured him. He already put His stamp of approval on Jeremiah and commissioned him to fulfill his God-given destiny. God desires to do the same for you. Be willing to walk in His ways, and God will begin to unfold His plan for your life.

Your Gift

I remember praying one morning, trying to figure out what direction God wanted me to walk in for my future. As I was praying the Lord revealed to me the distinction between having a goal to accomplish and using my God-given gifts and talents for *His glory*. You see, God has placed gifts in each of us for His purposes. This is a very important concept that we Christians sometimes miss. We get so busy trying to fulfill our destiny that we miss the importance of our purpose. Yes, we have a destiny, and yes we have a "call" on our lives. But the goal is for God's name to be lifted up, not ours. It is all about the gifts and talents that are in us for *His use*.

I was focusing on the wrong things. I was focusing on the by-products of the gift, and not on the gift that resides in me for His purpose. Be careful you do not focus on the fruit of your gift and not the gift itself. For example, if a pastor of a large church has a gift to teach people marvelous biblical truths but begins to focus on his great speaking ability, he will lose focus on his gift of teaching. His focus will shift to his own charisma to move audiences. Sure he may have a good speaking ability, but it is only a by-product of his main gift—teaching. If he switches his focus from teaching and becomes enamored by entertaining large audiences, he will be using his gifts to benefit himself rather than to glorify God. We must understand that when God places a gift within us it is to be used to fulfill God's own purposes.

Many times people prostitute the gift that is in them. What I mean by this is they take the talents and abilities God has placed in them and use it to enlarge their own ego or to get rich, instead of investing that gift into God's plan for their lives.

There have been many times I have told God, "My life is yours. You ordain my steps. You open doors that no man could shut and shut doors that no man can open. I unequivocally want your will." I knew God had the best outcome for me, and I did not want to interrupt God's plan for my life. I have been tempted to consider other career paths, but I felt a nudging not to go in that direction. It is important to always keep an open heart toward God. His plan will bring you the most joy to your life.

You Are Unique

I want to focus on your uniqueness, because this ties into your purpose. We know that there are no two people alike.

No two sets of fingerprints are alike. We know that no two people have the same DNA patterns, and I want you to know that no one else can fulfill your purpose. I do not care if people look at you and doubt that you will ever amount to much. That is a lie that needs to be replaced with truth. You are valuable and greatly loved. Listen to what God has to say about you.

> The LORD your God has chosen you to be a people for Himself, a special treasure above all the peoples on the face of the earth. The LORD did not set His love on you nor choose you because you were more in number than any other people, for you were the least of all peoples; but because the LORD loves you.
>
> —DEUTERONOMY 7:6–8

Understand that God is saying, "I don't love you because you are strong or a good person, but I love you because you are you. You are special."

He has made and designed you with wonderful abilities and talents that He will use for His purposes. We do not have to prove anything to God to persuade Him to take an interest in us. People are the ones who judge each other by what someone has accomplished or overcome, but God looks at the heart. He is happy about us even while we are in the process of accomplishing or overcoming. It is God who knew at the beginning of our situation that we would get to the end of that situation. God has confidence in you because He designed you. He knows the potential that resides in you even when your behavior is not so great.

He has made and designed you with wonderful abilities and talents that He will use for His purposes.

Timing

I would be at great fault if I did not take a moment and tell you God's timing is not always our timing. I opened this chapter by telling you that God revealed to me in 1994 that I would write a book, but that goal was not actually fulfilled until December 2003—nine long years later! We all go through seasons of growth. God knows just the right time to begin to open the right doors for us to walk in. The good news is that God is faithful. Those desires that burn in your heart, if God placed them there, they will come to fruition. This is a key to staying encouraged during hard times. Do not be as concerned with *when* your purpose will come to pass, as you are with knowing your life has meaning.

Be careful to enjoy where you are while you are on your way to where you are going. I remember many times I felt very low because I had many limitations in my life. I would wonder how I could fulfill my destiny with all my limitations. Eventually I got to the point where I started to make decisions based on what I felt was in my heart. I began to not care if I had limitations. I was determined that they would not stop me from walking in my purpose. The good news is my limitations do not define who I am any longer. My value is not determined by my strengths and weakness nor by my successes and failures, but my value is determined by the very fact that I was born! Your value is not determined by your work but rather by the fact that God created you. You are His child and He loves you just because you are you!

SET GOALS

Set some goals for yourself. It is good to have at least an outline of what you would like to become, how you would like to impact the people around you, where you would like to be in your life in one year from now, even five or ten years from now. Every year my husband and I sit down and write out personal goals for ourselves and financial goals for our family. At the end of the year we look back to see what was accomplished and what was not, what was God's will for our lives and what was not.

If you do not have any goals then you are not able to make decisions that will enable you to move closer to your destiny. Setting goals makes for a wonderfully encouraged life, and it helps in your decision-making process to know there is meaning and purpose to your life!

NOTES

_____

_____

_____

_____

_____

_____

_____

_____

_____

_____

_____

_____

_____

_____

_____

_____

_____

For the word of God is living and powerful, and sharper than any two-edged sword, piercing even to the division of soul and spirit, and of joints and marrow, and is a discerner of the thought and intents of the heart.

—HEBREWS 4:12

CHAPTER 6

Promises to Pursue

T HE ONLY WAY to live an encouraged life is to replace the lie with the truth. You may ask the question: What is truth and where can it be found? Truth is found in the Bible. There are no absolutes in this world except for the spoken Word of God. Whether or not you believe the Bible is God's Word is between you and God. I believe we all have a measure of faith to believe, but the decision is yours. I have witnessed God's Word change my life.

---

*The only way to live an
encouraged life is to replace
the lie with the truth.*

The goal of this chapter is to help line your thinking up with God's thinking. This is a key to experiencing true joy in your life. I am going to list scriptures that have changed my life. There were times when I would have to remind myself daily of these truths. I challenge you to test your thinking against God's Word. If your thinking lines up with God's Word, then you are probably living an encouraged life. If your thinking does not line up with God's Word, then you probably are not living an encouraged life.

In the Book of Hebrews we learn of the divine authority of God's Word.

> For the word of God is living and powerful, and sharper than any two-edged sword, piercing even to the division of soul and spirit, and of joints and marrow, and is a discerner of the thoughts and intents of the heart.
>
> —HEBREWS 4:12

God's Word is able to show us who we really are and why we do the things we do. He already knows what we think before we actually think it, and He sees into our hearts. Thank God He does not love us based on how "good" we are, but He loves us because we are His.

In the Gospel of John 8:32 Jesus said, "You shall know the truth, and the truth shall make you free." The word *know* in the Hebrew means "to recognize the truth by personal experience."[8] I have experienced change through the power of God's Word. The lies I once believed about myself have been replaced with the truth of how God sees me. There is an old adage that says, "On your journey to finding out who God is, you will inadvertently discover who you are."

The following scriptures are ones that I personally have applied to my life. These scriptures have been posted throughout my home, in my car, and in my purse. I have even carried them with me on vacation. They went wherever I went. Get ready. It is my prayer that after you read these truths, you will be encouraged, energized, confident, and expectant. Consider this a self-test. After each scripture ask yourself the question, "Do I really believe this statement to be true?" Feel free to copy these scriptures and hang them up somewhere where you will read them often!

> Whoever listens to me will dwell safely,
> And will be secure, without fear or evil.
>
> —PROVERBS 1:33

> For I am God, and not man,
> The Holy One in your midst;
> And I will not come with terror.
>
> —HOSEA 11:9

69

An Encouraging Word

I will not forget you.
See, I have inscribed you on the palms of My
   hands.

—Isaiah 49:15–16

As one whom his mother comforts,
So I will comfort you;
And you shall be comforted.

—Isaiah 66:13

For I, the Lord your God, will hold your right
   hand,
Saying to you, "Fear not, I will help you."

—Isaiah 41:13

You are all fair, my love,
And there is no spot in you.

—Song of Solomon 4:7

Be still, and know that I am God.

—Psalm 46:10

Behold I am the Lord, the God of all flesh. Is
there anything too hard for Me?

—Jeremiah 32:27

"Shall I bring to the time of birth, and not cause
delivery?" says the Lord.

—Isaiah 66:9

So I will restore to you the years that the
    swarming locust has eaten,
The crawling locust,
The consuming locust,
And the chewing locust.

—JOEL 2:25

"For I will restore health to you
And heal you of your wounds," says the LORD.

—JEREMIAH 30:17

Call to me and I will answer you and tell you
great and unsearchable things you do not
know.

—JEREMIAH 33:3, NIV

I have heard your prayer, I have seen your tears;
surely I will heal you.

—2 KINGS 20:5

Do not be afraid nor dismayed because of this
great multitude, for the battle is not yours, but
God's.

—2 CHRONICLES 20:15

"Comfort, yes, comfort My people!"
Says your God.
"Speak comfort to Jerusalem, and cry out to
    her,
That her warfare is ended,
That her iniquity is pardoned."

—Isaiah 40:1–2

Instead of your shame you shall have double honor.

—Isaiah 61:7

Oh, taste and see that the Lord is good;
Blessed is the man who trusts in Him!

—Psalm 34:8

No evil shall befall you,
Nor shall any plague come near your dwelling.

—Psalm 91:10

For you did not receive the spirit of bondage again to fear, but you received the Spirit of adoption by whom we cry out, "Abba Father" [daddy].

—Romans 8:15

He has not dealt with us according to our sins,
Nor punished us according to our iniquities.

—Psalm 103:10

You shall weep no more. He will be very gracious to you at the sound of your cry; when He hears it, He will answer you.

—ISAIAH 30:19

For the LORD God is a sun and shield;
The LORD will give grace and glory;
No good thing will He withhold
From those who walk uprightly.

—PSALM 84:11

Those who trust in the LORD
Are like Mount Zion,
Which cannot be moved, but abides forever.
As the mountains surround Jerusalem,
So the LORD surrounds His people.

—PSALM 125:1–2

He delivered me because He delighted in me.

—PSALM 18:19

Rest in the LORD, and wait patiently for Him.

—PSALM 37:7

Let us not grow weary while doing good, for in due season we shall reap if we do not lose heart.

—GALATIANS 6:9

They reel to and fro, and stagger like a
    drunken man,

And are at their wits' end.
Then they cry out to the LORD in their trouble,
And He brings them out of their distresses.
He calms the storm,
So that its waves are still.

—PSALM 107:27–29

· In the multitude of my anxieties within me,
Your comforts delight my soul.

—PSALM 94:19

Draw near to God and He will draw near to
you.

—JAMES 4:8

[There is] a time to laugh [play, rejoice].

—ECCLESIASTES 3:4

All of the above scriptures can be life changing. But if
you don't know the One making the promises, they will
have little effect in your life. If you don't already have a
relationship with God take a moment right now to ask
Jesus to come into your heart and forgive you of your sins.
Ask God to reveal Himself and His Word to you.

I did this when I was twenty years old. I was at college
and I met this woman who worked at the college. She
seemed to have so much joy. I told her I wanted that same
joy. She told me I too could have joy and peace by having
a relationship with Jesus Christ. So that evening I prayed
and asked God to forgive me of my sins and to come into

my life. Being someone who suffered from intense worry and anxiety, it was the best decision I ever made.

That evening after I prayed someone knocked on my dorm room door. It was a girl from Puerto Rico who spoke very little English. She had only been at the college a short time studying English. Imagine my surprise when she came in with her Bible right after I just had this encounter with God. She had some verses in her Bible highlighted in yellow. One verse was: "Don't worry about anything; instead, pray about everything" (Phil. 4:6, NLT). I was shocked that God cared enough about me to send someone with a message that gave me an answer to what I was facing at that moment. This is how I have found God to be in my life. He has met my needs when I thought there was no way out of a situation. He always provided a way to go through a difficulty, or He has made a way out of a difficulty. Jesus has proven Himself to be faithful time and time again.

With all the threats of terror that are going on in the world today, I am encouraged to know that there is a God who holds the whole world in the palm of His hands. I know each night I fall asleep under the watchful eye of God. I would not trade the peace and tranquillity that comes from having a relationship with a personal God.

THE GREATEST PROMISE TO PURSUE

I walked through most of my life with a broken heart, with sadness in my soul. Sometimes that sadness would surface and sometimes I would be going about life as usual. As I mentioned earlier, my life has been like an onion. Layer by layer, hurts have been peeled away and replaced by the love of God. At the root of most emotional problems is a lack of feeling loved and cherished by someone. It does not matter if you struggle with depression, anxiety, drug addiction, alcoholism, eating disorders, or anger, the fact remains that we all need to know we are loved and wanted. The Lord speaks to us through His Word saying, "Yes, I have loved you with an everlasting love; therefore with lovingkindness I have drawn you, again I will build you, and you shall be rebuilt" (Jer. 31:3–4). There is such comfort in this verse. The greatest promise to pursue is God's love. People will both disappoint and delight us, but God is much more stable than people. He will always have our best in mind.

God enjoys turning those negative situations around for our good. I'm reminded of a scripture that says, "For the eyes of the Lord run to and fro throughout the whole earth, to show Himself strong on behalf of those whose heart is loyal to Him" (2 Chron. 16:9). This verse is telling us that God actually looks to bless His people. He looks to do good to those who love Him. I find many times that His Word surprises me, because it is so different from my original perceptions of what God should be like. This is why it is so important to renew our minds with His truth. We cannot fail when we trust in an unfailing God!

NOTES

For I know the thoughts that I think toward you, says the Lord, thoughts of peace and not of evil, to give you a future and a hope.

—JEREMIAH 29:11

CHAPTER 7

The Last Word

I WEAVED THROUGHOUT THIS book the fact that I have struggled with anxiety. For years I have battled anxious, negative thinking. People who worry and have anxiety think too much, and that gets us into trouble. I am learning to decrease my worry time and enjoy my life. The most important thing I have learned concerning anxiety is to take my self-defeating thoughts and turn them around for good. I have had to really work hard at this, but it has been worth it. I refuse to waste any more time worrying about something that may never happen. I want to share with you some helpful hints that have helped me reduce the amount of time I spend worrying.

STRESS

Stress can come in many forms. The definition of *stress* is "to press, to urge, to distress, to put to difficulties."[9] How many of us live under constant pressure? Some of it we self-induce. Let me give you a recent example. I had a very busy day planned. It was a Saturday morning, and by 10:00 a.m., I was already overwhelmed by my day. I could feel my body tense up and my mind was racing in a million different directions. I felt I had several tasks I needed to accomplish in one day. I did not know what to do first. I could not enjoy anything I was doing, because I was in such a hurry to move onto the next project.

Looking back, I can easily recognize that I needed to take time out and make some changes in my schedule. I was overwhelmed, but I proceeded into my day, trying to accomplish everything on my "to do" list. My family and I had an errand to go on, and we were driving someplace. I could feel tension turning into intense anxiety. The kind of anxiety that makes you so uncomfortable you want to turn around, go home, and put the sheets over your head and say, "Enough! I needed to rest!" I proceeded with accomplishing that errand, all the while telling myself the truth, "Luann, you know you're stressed out right now, that's why you feel so uncomfortable and anxious, but when you get home you're going to make some changes in your day." This helped ease my anxiety level, and eventually the anxiety subsided. The anxiety decreased because I began to encourage myself. I began to speak to myself in a way that brought peace rather than pressure. When I got home from that errand and throughout the rest of the day, I made sure that I reduced my "to do" list, and that evening I went out and did something fun!

I have learned stress can be a starting point for other negative emotions. Maybe when you get stressed, instead of getting anxious perhaps you get angry, depressed, or irritable. Maybe you eat too much, drink too much, or withdraw from other people. The point is to recognize the stress for what it is and then do something about it. Watch carefully how you speak to yourself. Make sure you are encouraging yourself rather than dragging yourself down to a pit. Make some changes in your day like I had to. Perhaps you need to make some serious lifestyle changes. Whatever the case is do not stay depressed and discouraged because you have stress.

DEEP ISSUES OF THE HEART

Another area that needs to be addressed is hurtful events that can happen in our lives. There are many people who appear to be perfectly content and happy with their life on the surface, but if you could see deep into their heart you would find a wounded individual. I *used* to be that person. On the surface my life seemed "normal," but inside I was a mess. There were events that happened in my life and decisions that I made that negatively affected me. I want you to learn that it is hard to live an encouraged life when you're bleeding emotionally. I have found in my own experience that I needed to seek counseling, write in a journal, and confide in a good friend. I think most of the time we would rather not talk about painful events. I can tell you from personal experience that it is when I confronted some of those painful events that I experienced healing and restoration. It appears to be easier to simply ignore painful areas of our lives, but I can assure you it is very difficult to stay encouraged when you are broken inside.

You could read all the self-help books available, but until you get really honest with yourself and really honest with God, you are only going to be putting a Band-Aid on your wounds. I remember once as I was writing in a journal about a painful event in my life, I felt like I was tiptoeing around a huge scab. Nonetheless, I continued to bring those issues out into the light. A wise counselor once told me to write about an event until it doesn't bother me anymore. I can honestly tell you today that there are certain events in my life that do not have a "hold" on my life like they used to.

A friend of mine tried to convince me that I needed to attend a weekend retreat called Rachel's Vineyard. She said this retreat would change my life. I put her off for a year. I finally reluctantly went to this retreat and she was right, my life was changed. Words cannot express the impact this retreat had on my life. Sometimes we need to be out of our routines and away from the distractions of life, and just focus on healing our pain with the help and comfort of Jesus Christ.

The point is, when God is tugging on your heart to get some help for a particular area of your life, don't put it off for a year like I did. My prayer for you right now, as you are reading this book, is that you will be restored and made whole again. In Joel 2:25 God says to His people, "So I will restore to you the years that the swarming locust has eaten, the crawling locust and the chewing locust." The word *restore* in the Hebrew language means "to be safe in mind, body, and estate." God is saying to you right now that His will for your life is that you be well in three areas: your mind, your body, and your possessions.

Take a few moments at the end of this section and write down any areas that you feel you need counseling in, or areas that you feel you need to confide in a good friend. Don't let time pass without healing your brokenness. I can only speak from my experience, that confronting hurts from my past has led me to a greater peace in my present!

REST, RELAX, AND REFRESH

Even as I write the three Rs (rest, relax, refresh) I must tell you this is a fairly new concept to me. I have recently learned of the incredible power of balance—balancing work and rest. At times I get so involved and excited about a project that I'm working on that I neglect the idea of "stopping to smell the roses." This is called relaxing. Find a hobby or anything that you enjoy that causes you to relax. If all I ever did was stay busy and on a schedule, I would become tired and irritable. If I were to continually relax and rest, I would be bored and restless. If all I did was function as a caregiver or one who puts out fires, I would run out of physical and emotional energy. There needs to be balance and a time for replenishment and rejuvenation for your spirit, mind, and body. It really does not matter what profession we are in or what our daily schedules are, we need to schedule in some time to relax. I look at it this way: if I were to give, give, give and never be refreshed or restored in my spirit, mind, and body, I would be no good for anyone. Remember stress can result in other negative emotions. When we are rest, we insulate ourselves from stress.

Go Play

I have a saying on one of my walls that says, "Success is knowing when to stop and play." I bought this and hung it up to remind myself to have fun and get out and enjoy life. If you can't think of ways to have fun, just get around children and observe them. When kids are playing, they are carefree. They do not have much to worry about. Their purpose is to play.

What are some hobbies you enjoy doing? Perhaps you could find something that your whole family can do together to have fun. My husband and I play tennis and are teaching our kids to play. This is something that is fun for our whole family. Figure out what makes you feel carefree. Now, go out and do it!

The Book of Proverbs says, "A merry heart does good, like medicine" (17:22). Having fun is good for us. God knows better than anyone how we are wired, and He said in His Word a long time ago that when we laugh it is like a medicine for our bodies. This is truth, and it is truth that sets us free.

HALF FULL OR HALF EMPTY?

How would you describe your life? Is the glass half full or half empty? If your answer is half empty you're probably focusing on the wrong things in life. We all could tell of bitter experiences and tragedies in our lives. But I am encouraging you to look at your life positively, with a "glass-half-full" attitude. What is right in your life? What are you proud of? Don't just read the questions, but really think about how blessed you are. The next time you are tempted to get discouraged remind yourself of what is right in your life.

I can recall being in a very low point in my life, and I would remind myself of two little children that were right in my life. My children are the most precious blessings in my life. Many times they have brought joy into my life.

Take a few moments and write down at the end of this chapter a list of all the blessings in your life. Sometimes writing things down helps us to remember them. When you become thankful for all the blessings you already have, you will stay encouraged.

I know people who always have something negative to say. Their lives are always half empty. They are usually complaining about the latest tragedy in their lives, how someone has wronged them, or a constant physical aliment in their body. Rarely does anything positive come out of their mouths. This can rob their quality of life, as well as the quality of life of those around them. I do not like to be around people like this, because I do not want to walk down that path of negativity. We are only on this earth for a certain number of years, and I want to enjoy the life I have been given.

Believe

Another important key to staying encouraged is faith. Hebrews 11:1 gives a great definition for faith: "Faith is the substance of things hoped for, the evidence of things not seen." This is the idea of believing the good even when you cannot see the good. It is in difficult times that we must continue to believe for a positive outcome even when we cannot see the end result or the way out of our struggles. If you do not know any promises from God for your life, go back to chapter six and read some of God's promises to you.

A very special friend wrote a poem for me during a period in my life when my world was crashing in on all sides. I remember very vividly this time in my life. It was during the winter months, and we were standing in the grocery store talking. I didn't have to say much to her, and yet she knew things were really rough for me. She told me that God had put a poem on her heart to encourage me. I believe this poem was not written just to encourage me, but it was written to encourage and inspire many others. Be blessed as you read these inspiring words. The poem is called "Believe."[10]

> I believe in your God-given dreams
> The insurmountable is not always what it
> seems.
>
> I believe in your genuine heart
> For the Lord knows it's the most precious part.
>
> I believe in your desire to hope
> It is the strength with which you continue to
> cope.
>
> I believe you are a seeker of truth
> Even if it is not the beliefs of your youth.
>
> I believe you are a vessel of glory
> And when the tale is told it will be a beautiful
> story.
>
> I believe in your spirit of peace
> For when frustrations abound His control
> does not cease.
>
> I believe that God does care
> And He sees all the scars your soul does bear.

And in His infinite wisdom and grace,
We have the opportunity to seek His holy face.

I believe in your God-given dreams,
As the light of your destiny through the dark-
ness beams.

—Susan Gygax

Your destiny will begin to beam as you trust in God's
unconditional love for you and as you begin to replace old
negative thinking for the truth of God's Word. You are not
a mistake. You were put on this earth for a purpose. You
are valuable and important. If no one has over told you, I
am telling you right now. You have a destiny that only you
can fulfill.

> *Your destiny will begin to beam
> as you trust in God's uncondi-
> tional love for you.*

As I close this discussion on encouragement, I would
like to leave you with the same thoughts I opened with:

1. The trial you have been facing will become
   your greatest stepping stone.

2. Your pain will heal.

3. Your emotional struggle will turn into a powerhouse of strength for you.

4. Your loved one will one day cease to break your heart.

5. Your addiction will dismantle.

6. The raging crisis will settle down.

7. Your financial burden will be supplied.

8. Your aspiration or dream will be attained.

9. Your broken relationship will be healed.

10. You can lose weight.

11. You will come out of depression.

12. You do have tremendous value and worth.

13. You will find comfort even in the loss of your loved one.

14. Anything is possible if you believe.

I want you to know that if your situation looks bleak, your season will change. Mine did. You are the only one who can allow encouragement to come into your life. Do not look to other people to fulfill your needs. Look to God as your source. Because God gave each of us the power to choose, we are responsible for our own happiness. Regardless of our circumstances, we can choose to make the joy of the Lord our strength.

There is one final scripture that has become a signature scripture for my life. This final truth has been an instrument of great encouragement and expectation in my life.

> Now to Him who is able to do exceedingly abundantly above all that we ask or think, according to the power that works in us.
>
> —Ephesians 3:20

I am expecting God to far exceed even my greatest plans. I have seen God do much more than I expected many times, and I am looking forward to watching my obstacles turn into great opportunities. Don't ever give up or give in. Stay the course until you see the light at the end of your tunnel. And don't ever forget to speak an encouraging word!

NOTES

_____

_____

_____

_____

_____

_____

_____

_____

_____

_____

_____

_____

_____

_____

_____

_____

_____

Conclusion

I T HAS BEEN my prayer that this book will be a starting point for you. A starting point for you to begin to
see your problems as your stepping stones. I want to
encourage you that it will take time and much repetition
for you to change your negative perspectives into a positive point of view.

It is no accident that you have this book in your hands. I
believe you're at a crossroads right now. Either you're going
to begin to accept God's word as the truth for your life or
you're going to continue to live in discouragement. If there
are certain situations in your life that greatly hinder you,
you may want to research scriptures that will encourage
you, or talk to a good friend, or even seek out a Christian

counselor. Whatever path you need to take, start today!

Begin to evaluate your quality of life; is there room for improvement?

Watch carefully what you are thinking about, and what comes out of your mouth; is it positive concerning your future or are you complaining and being negative?

Are you going to God daily and asking Him to forgive you and are you forgiving those who have hurt you?

Do you have hope for your tomorrows? Hope will be the force that propels you into a good destiny.

Do you recognize that you are extremely valuable and there is no one on this earth that is as special as you are? You have a purpose that only you can fulfill.

Don't forget to remind yourself of powerful truths found in God's word. You may have to hang scriptures around your house and other places where you will continually read them.

Remember to bring some balance into your life. Balance your work with play. Find a hobby or a sport that you enjoy, read something that makes you laugh. Go outside and look at the beauty around you. Fix your eyes on living life to the fullest.

Make up your mind to be encouraged!

I leave you with one last powerful principle that has brought peace into my life. This principle is on forgiveness. In fact this is so important to me that I promised God wherever I had an opportunity to speak to audiences that I would teach them the following principle. It is found in Matthew 18:23–35:

Therefore the kingdom of heaven is like a certain king who wanted to settle accounts with his servants. And when he had begun to settle accounts, one was brought to him who owed him ten thousand talents. But as he was not able to pay, his master commanded that he be sold, with his wife and children and all that he had, and that payment be made. The servant therefore fell down before him, saying, master have patience with me and I will pay you all. [This is what we say to God.] Then the master of that servant was moved with compassion, released him, and forgave him the debt. [This is how God would respond to us.]

But that servant went out and found one of his fellow servants who owed him a hundred denarii; and he laid hands on him and took him by the throat, saying, pay me what you owe. So his fellow servant fell down at his feet and begged him, saying, have patience with me, and I will pay you all. And he would not but went and threw him into prison till he should pay the debt. [Unlike God, this is how we typically respond to those who have wronged us.]

So when his fellow servants saw what had been done, they were very grieved, and came and told the master all that had been done. Then his master, after he had called him, said to him, you wicked servant! I forgave you all that debt because you begged me. Should you not also have had compassion on your fellow servant, just as I had compassion on you? And his master was angry, and delivered him to the torturers until he should pay all that was due to him. *So my heavenly father also will do to you if each of you, from his heart, does not forgive his brother his trespasses.*

The message in this parable is that God compassionately forgives us, yet we fiercely refuse to forgive others. What we don't realize is that there are consequences to *us* if we do not forgive. Just like the scripture says we will be delivered to the torturers. The goal is to live at peace, but there will be no peace of mind for us when we choose not to forgive. This parable can also be applied to us when we choose not to forgive ourselves. This is a powerful tool to living an encouraged life.

You do not have to waste any more of your precious life being discouraged.

If I can learn to live at peace amidst troublesome circumstances, so can you. Just as I have overcome discouragement so can you! And finally just as my season of winter has turned into a new season of restoration, know that this too will happen for you!

Be encouraged!

Notes

CHAPTER 1
YOUR QUALITY OF LIFE

1. *American Dictionary of the English Language: Noah Webster 1828 Edition Facsimile* (Chesapeake, VA: Foundation for American Christian Education, 2000).

CHAPTER 2
YOU ARE WHAT YOU SPEAK

1. John C. Maxwell, *Thinking for a Change: 11 Ways Highly Successful People Approach Life and Work* (New York: Warner Faith, 2003), 12.

CHAPTER 3
YOU DESERVE TO BE HAPPY

1. *Life Application Bible*, (Colorado Springs, CO: Zondervan, 1983).
2. *American Dictionary of the English Language.*

CHAPTER 4
ARE YOU HOPEFUL?

1. *American Dictionary of the English Language.*
2. *The Spirit-Filled Life Bible*, (Nashville, TN: Thomas Nelson Publishers, 1991), 1260.

CHAPTER 5
FULFILLING YOUR PURPOSE

1. *American Dictionary of the English Language.*

CHAPTER 6
PROMISES TO PURSUE

1. *The Spirit-Filled Life Bible*, (Nashville, TN: Thomas Nelson Publishers, 1991), 1589.

CHAPTER 7
THE LAST WORD

1. *American Dictionary of the English Language.*

ALSO AVAILABLE BY LUANN DUNNUCK:

The Timeless Treasure: A Commentary on the Song of Solomon

This book is a great Bible study guide to understanding the Song of Solomon. It may be used in groups or individually. *The Timeless Treasure* is a must for anyone who wrestles with doubting their own worth and value.

To contact Luann Dunnuck or to have her be a guest speaker at your organization please inquire at:

G&S Treasures
E-mail: GSTreasure@aol.com

Rachel's Vineyard Ministries

WEEKEND RETREATS FOR HEALING AFTER ABORTION

God's love, mercy, and healing bring restoration and hope to those who have suffered the loss of a child through abortion. *Rachel's Vineyard Retreats* are a beautiful way for women and men to come to terms of peace and healing with God, their babies, and with themselves. If you or anyone you know has been personally impacted by abortion, please contact the number below for referral to a *Rachel's Vineyard Retreat* in your area. Forty-three percent of women will have had at least one abortion by the age of 45. Let's do all we can to help these women be fully restored to Christ.

WWW.RACHELSVINEYARD.ORG
1-877-HOPE4ME

86 Hickory Hill Drive
Waterbury, CT 06708
(203) 574-1353

Email: angie_colella@yahoo.com

Women of Wisdom, Inc. is organized exclusively for charitable purposes; more specifically, the organization is dedicated to uniting women in need from all ethnic, religious, and economic backgrounds to provide a venue in which they can be encouraged and empowered spiritually and emotionally and receive the help and assistance they need to combat various struggles they may be going through.

Currently, WOW seeks to fulfill this mission by a monthly nondenominational gathering of women joining for fellowship and relationships designed to bring them together to share their interests, needs, hurts, and wants, with a guest speaker, music accompanist, and dinner. As funding allows, it is the desire of WOW to open a center for women where an array of services are provided such as support groups and workshops for issues such as depression, money management, parenting, childcare, nutrition, and drug and alcohol recovery. This center will seek to provide affordable Christian counseling for those needing one-on-one support. An element of this center would include training materials to help women better themselves, including a computer learning center, library, and a "Connections" program, which will connect people as resources and mentors for each other. The Women of Wisdom Center will also provide emergency services for families in need of clothing and an emergency food pantry. In long-term planning, WOW would also like to expand to include men and children in the various programs that will be instituted.